Rhythmic Training by Robert Starer

Also available is "Basic Rhythmic Training" which is a very elementary approach to rhythmic training for those with no prior knowledge. If you've already completed that book, turn to Chapter V in this book to continue your rhythmic training.

ISBN 978-0-88188-976-5

HAL•LEONARD® CORPORATION

7777 W. BLUEMOUND RD. P.O. BOX 13819 MILWAUKEE, WI 53213

Visit Hal Leonard Online at
www.halleonard.com

Foreword

This sequence of rhythmic exercises is a valuable addition to much needed material in music education. Its importance stems from contents that are well organized, consisting of simple elementary exercises that progress to complex drills, enabling students to reach a degree of proficiency, the kind that is, alas, sadly lacking in the general run of music students.

Though excellent treatises on musicianship exist, giving some examples of rhythmic problems, most of them do not have enough material for consistent drills. There are no short cuts to the mastery of one's craft. Conscientious teachers who have been writing their own drills have felt the need for such material in printed form.

Robert Starer's fine book is the answer to these needs. His approach is not only that of the teacher, but also that of the composer and performer. This happily is not a "method." It contains direct examples to be used as desired, with varied approaches and techniques. The main concern is its relationship to music, either read, performed or heard. Nothing could be more welcome to all music students and teachers.

Suzanne Bloch

Preface

The ability to transform visual symbols of rhythmic notation into time-dividing sounds is an acquired skill. It involves the coordination of physical, psychological, and musical factors and cannot, therefore, be accomplished by the simple act of comprehension. This book represents an attempt to develop and train the ability to read and perform musical rhythms accurately. It is not tied to any particular system of melodic ear-training and can be used in conjunction with any approach to sight-singing. It is intended for the classroom, for the private studio and for self-training.

The chapters are arranged in a sequence of increasing difficulty. Each chapter deals with a specific rhythmic situation. The problem is stated; a way to surmount it is proposed, and exercises are provided for practice purposes. The number of exercises in each chapter is designed to meet the needs of the average student. The brilliant student may need fewer. On the other hand it may be necessary to invent additional examples, modeled after those provided, for the less adept student. In some instances it may be advisable to divide the exercises into shorter segments. The student with previous experience will find his place in the book when he encounters his first difficulty.

No attempt has been made to shape these exercises into musical phrases or to give them form by repetition and development of rhythmic motives, since either procedure would tend to make the exercises memorizable by rote upon repetition in practicing.

In my experience as composer, performer and teacher I have come to the conclusion that inadequate grasp of rhythmic patterns is often the cause of poor sight-reading. It has also become increasingly apparent that lack of familiarity with 5 and 7 time and changing meters, particularly in the early stages of musical training, has contributed much to the unjustified fears of performing 20th-century music. This book was written in the hope of alleviating both of these situations.

Robert Starer

Acknowledgements

I would like to express my sincere gratitude to Suzanne Bloch, Dorothy Klotzman and Emile Serposs for their many helpful suggestions and to Lewis Roth and Bruce Howden for their editorial advice.

How to Use This Book

Throughout the first ten chapters of this book the upper line represents the rhythm the student should perform, the lower line is the pulse. The upper line may be sung, hummed or spoken on a neutral syllable; the lower line should be tapped by hand or foot, or it may be conducted. It is strongly recommended that the methods of execution be changed frequently, so that none becomes an exclusive habit. A metronome may be used for the lower line in the early chapters, but it is preferable for the student to produce the pulse himself. Eventually the lower line should only be "felt," that is, it should be done in silence.

While the upper line is always printed on a single note, a distinction between strong, medium strong, and weak beats in the pulse is indicated by placing the notes on different lines or spaces.

It is imperative that the student always differentiate clearly between strong and weak beats and not perform the pulse line as a sequence of identical beats.

The aim should be to execute the exercises at the fastest possible speed. To accomplish this, they should first be performed slowly, then repeated with gradually increased velocity until the individual's limit of capability is reached.

All students should be encouraged to invent their own examples, dealing with the specific problems set in the various chapters. This will strengthen the imprint of the rhythmic patterns involved on the student's mind. In class and in private instruction the exercises can also be used for dictation. Examples invented by the students often provide additional material for dictation. In classroom use it is also helpful to let individual students perform shorter segments, taking over from each other at predetermined intervals such as every three or four bars or every line. Another suggested teaching technique is for the teacher to insert deliberate errors into the examples he performs, challenging the student to find the mistakes and to correct them.

Contents

PRELIMINARY EXERCISES

Rhythmic Notation:

o = whole note, ♩ = half-note, ♩ = quarter-note, ♩. = dotted half-note
(The dot placed after any note adds to it one-half of its value.)

The Quarter-Note as pulse
Each unit of the pulse is called a beat.

Basic Notation:
♩ = 1 beat, ♩ = 2 beats, ♩. = 3 beats, **o** = 4 beats.

Compound Notation:

When two notes are tied, the second is treated as an addition to the first.

○ ♩ = 5 beats, ○ ♩ or ○• = 6 beats, ○ ♩• or ○•• = 7 beats,* ○ ○ or |○| = 8 beats.

*A second dot adds half the value of the first dot to the note. In this case the first dot added a half-note; the second, an additional quarter-note.

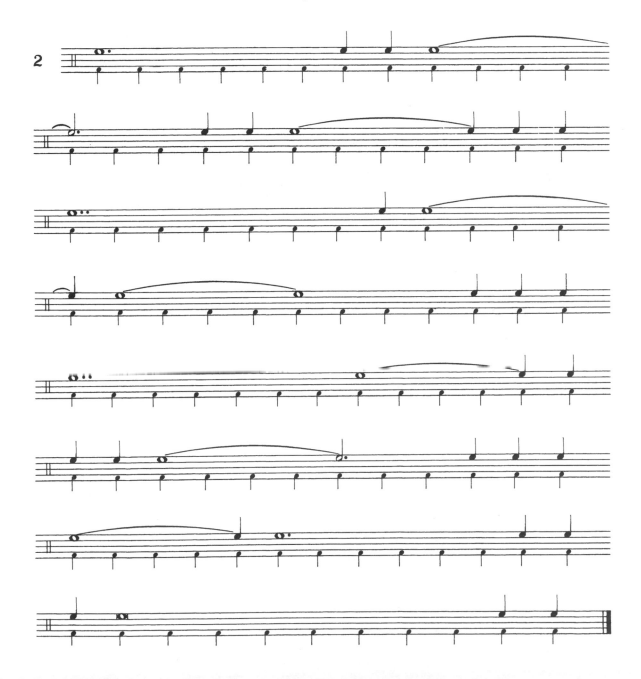

Notation of Silence:

Rests: ▬ = whole-rest ▬ = half-rest 𝄽 = quarter-rest

𝄽 = 1 beat ▬ = 2 beats ▬.* = 3 beats ▬ = 4 beats

*The dot after a rest functions identically with the dot after a note.

Rests must be performed with the same precision as notes; otherwise there would be no difference between 𝅗𝅥. and 𝅗𝅥 𝄽

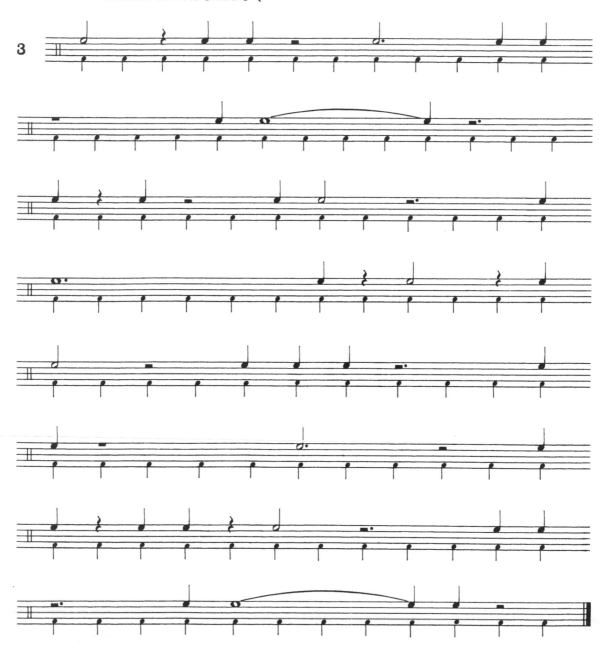

Chapter I

Rhythmic Organization, the Bar-line and Meter.

A vertical line divides the pulse into bars or measures. The first beat after each bar-line is always the downbeat (strong).

Two quarter-note beats per bar: $\frac{2}{4}$ meter =   Conductor's symbol: 1 ↓   2 ↑
                                            strong weak   downbeat upbeat

(A tie connecting two notes may go across the bar-line.)

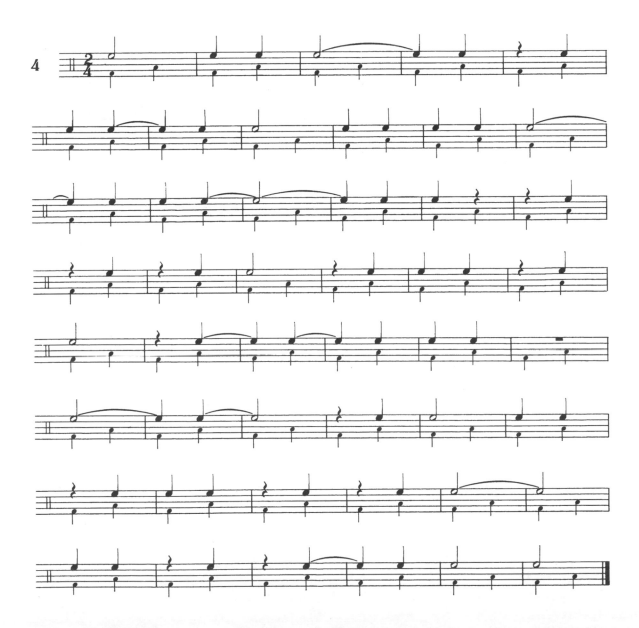

10

Three quarter-note beats per bar: **¾** meter =

strong   weak   weak

Five quarter-note beats per bar: $\frac{5}{4}$ is a combination of 3+2 or 2+3.

$\frac{5}{4}$ meter continued: mixing 2+3 and 3+2

9

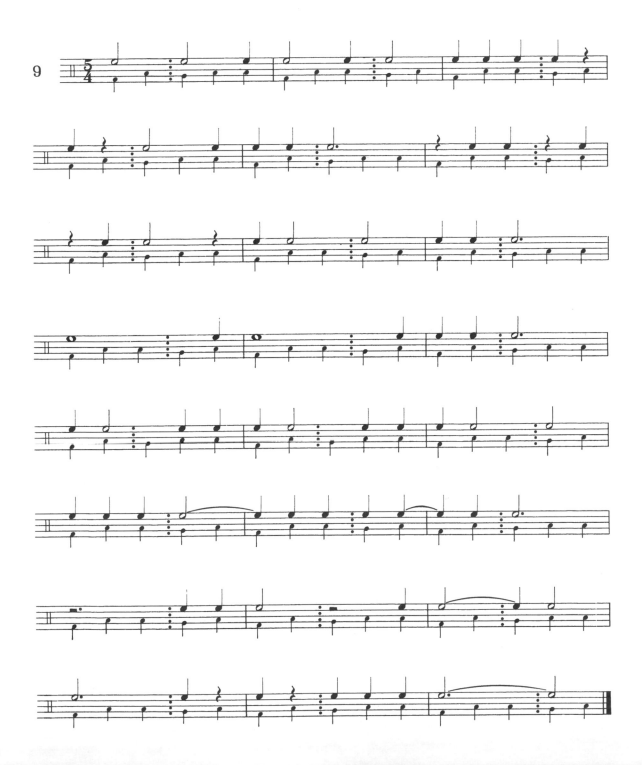

Six quarter-note beats per bar: $\frac{6}{4}$ meter,

Seven quarter-note beats per bar: $\frac{7}{4}$ is a combination of 4+3 or 3+4 or 2+3+2.

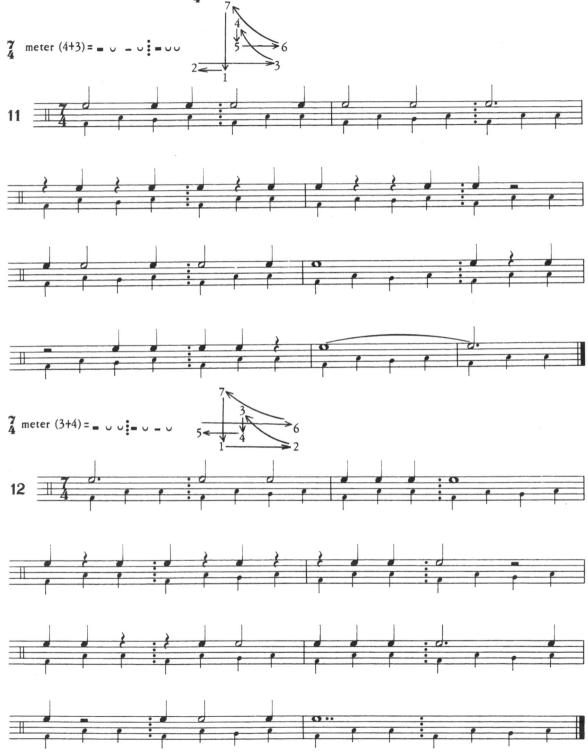

16

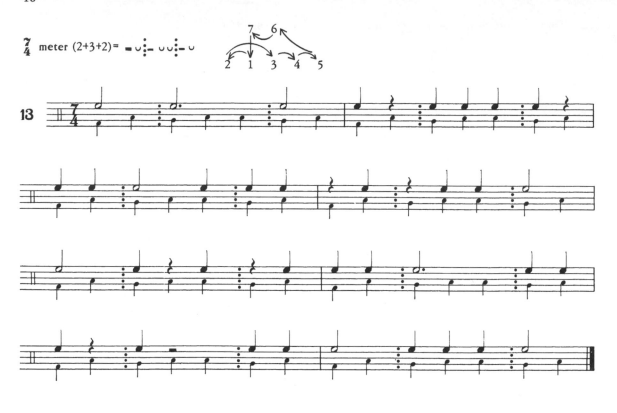

$\frac{7}{4}$ meter continued: mixing 4+3, 3+4 and 2+3+2.

Numbers larger than seven (beats per bar) are occasionally found in musical literature. They are rarely prime numbers such as 11 and 13, but mostly multiples of shorter numbers such as 9 (3×3) or 12 (4×3) and will be dealt with in later chapters.

Changing Meters

Chapter II

Dividing the Beat into Two Equal Parts
The Eighth-Note

Notation: The eighth-note can be notated ♪ ♪ or ♫ ; also ♬♬

$\frac{2}{4}$ meter = ■ ∪   (see No.4 for conductor's symbol)

Notation: The eighth-rest ♪

Notation: ♩♩‿♩♩ is usually notated ♪♩ ♪ Such an ''off-beat'' rhythm pattern is called syncopation. It can also be created by the use of ties and rests.

Notation: ♩. The dotted quarter-note equals three eighth-notes or one and a half quarter-note beats.

A musical composition can begin on an upbeat rather than on a downbeat. This upbeat may be an eighth or a quarter-note. In order to perform the upbeat precisely, it is wise to establish the pulse clearly before beginning.

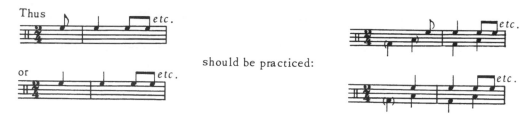

should be practiced:

Notation: usually the value of the upbeat is subtracted from the last bar.

3/4 meter = ▬ ∪ ∪

21

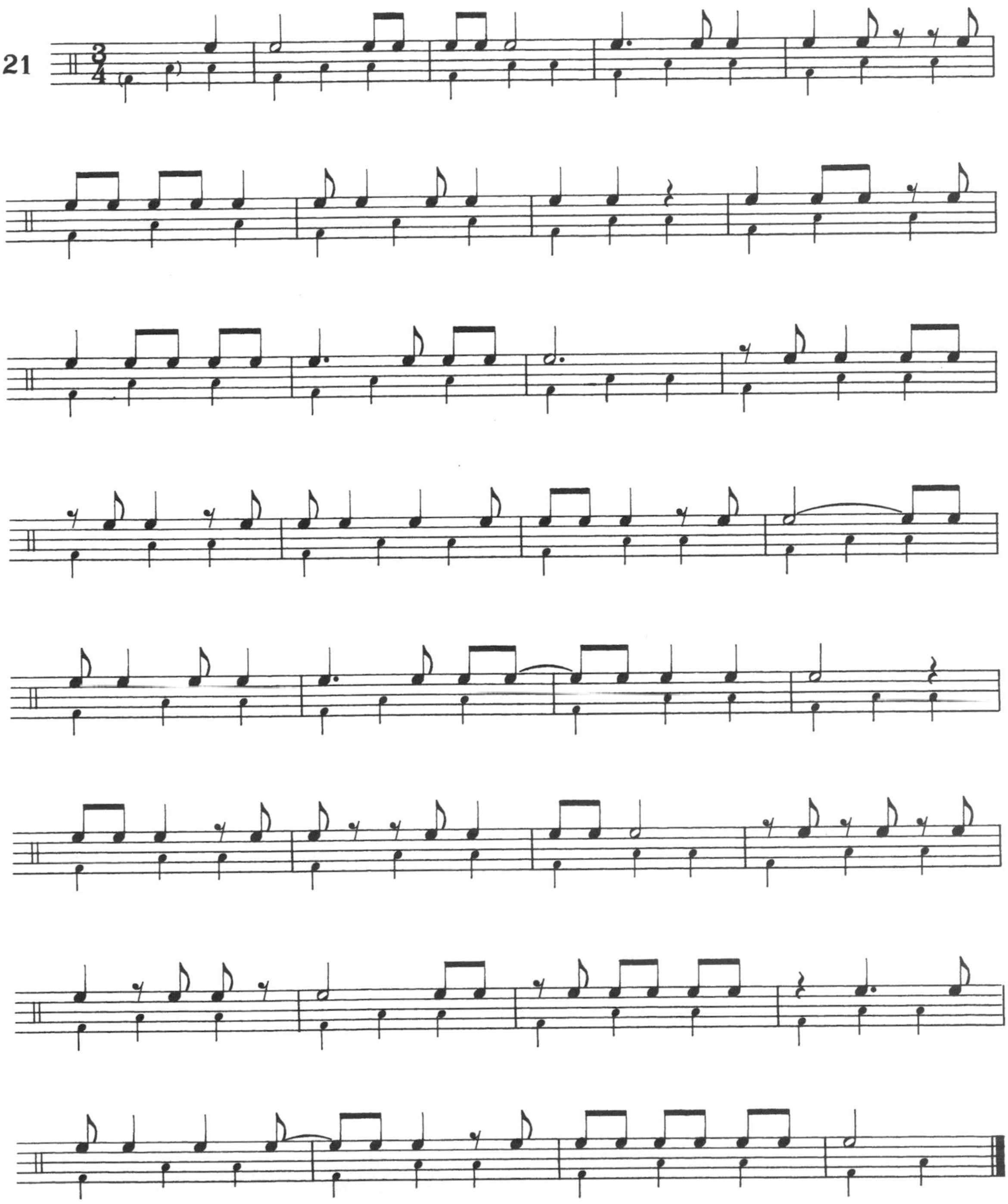

$\frac{5}{4}$ meter (3+2 or 2+3) = – ∪ ∪ ⁝ – ∪ or – ∪ ⁝ – ∪ ∪

23

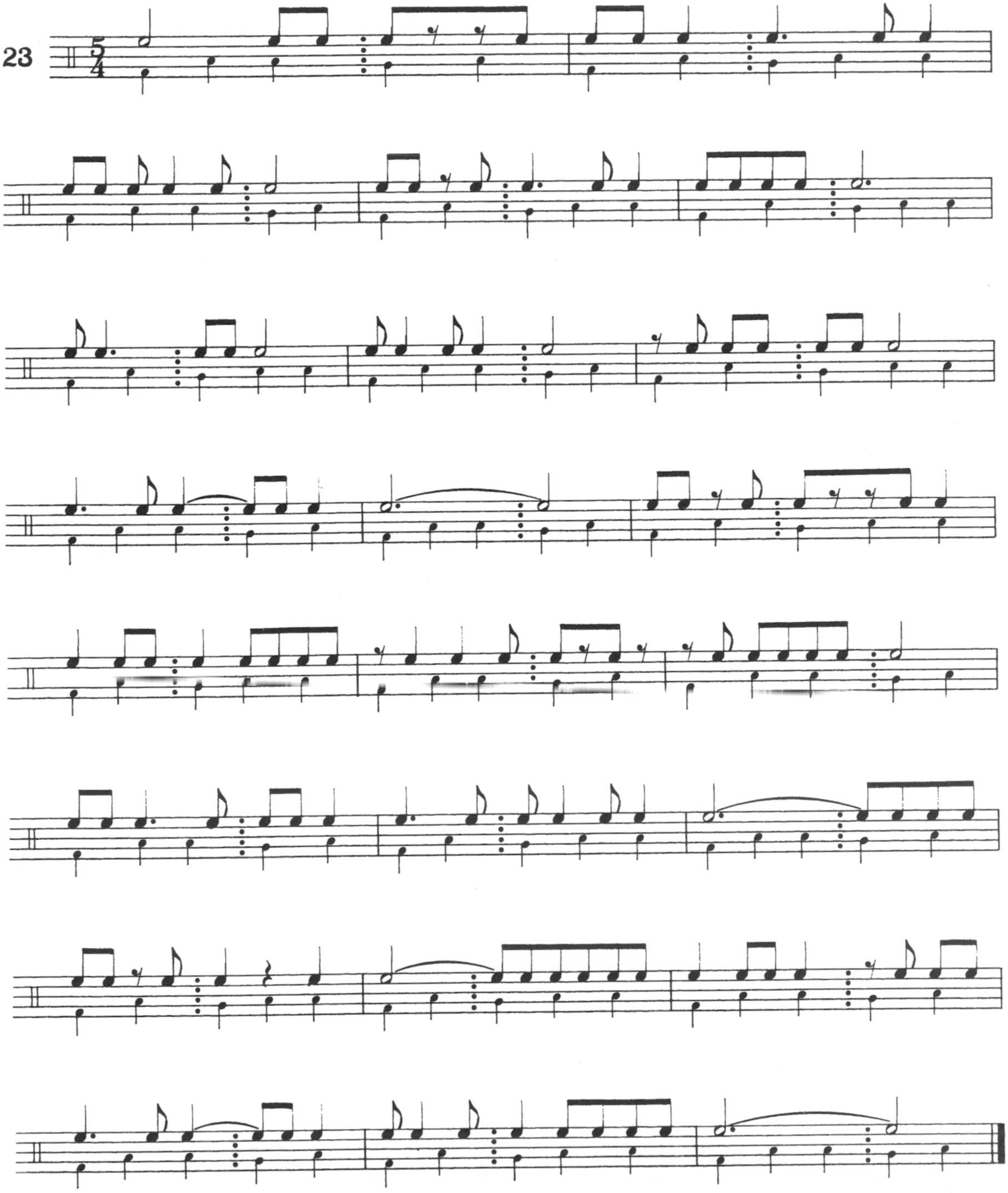

$\frac{6}{4}$ meter (3+3 or 2+2+2)= ▬ ◡ ◡ ▬ ◡ ◡ or ▬ ◡ ┊ ▬ ◡ ┊ ▬ ◡

24

Changing Meters.

Chapter III
Dividing the Beat into Three Equal Parts
The Triplet

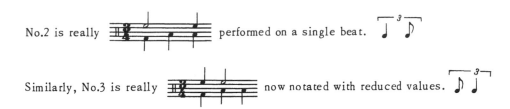

Three basic patterns: 1.   2.   3.

These basic patterns should be practiced separately. In order to acquire facility with numbers 2 and 3 it should be noted that they differ from previously practiced material only in notation and in their relationship to the pulse.

No.2 is really [notation] performed on a single beat. [notation]

Similarly, No.3 is really [notation] now notated with reduced values. [notation]

Notation: When a composition makes extensive use of the triple divided beat it is often notated with a dotted quarter-note as pulse. In this notation ♩.=1 beat; ♩.=2 beats; ♩. ♩.=3 beats; o.=4 beats.

Thus:

can be notated:

To the listener the two versions will sound identical.

Similarly:

can be notated:

$\frac{4}{4}$ can be notated as $\frac{12}{8}$; $\frac{5}{4}$ as $\frac{15}{8}$ etc.

Throughout this chapter both forms of notation will be practiced.

28

$\frac{2}{4}$ meter

27

$\frac{6}{8}$ meter

28

30

4/4 meter

31

12/8 meter

32

Changing Meters

Changing Meters

Chapter IV

Dividing the Beat into Four Equal Parts
The Sixteenth-Note

Notation: the sixteenth-note can be notated ♪♪♪♪ or ♬♬

Six basic patterns: 1. ♬♬   2. ♩♫   3. ♫♩   4. ♩.♫   5. ♫♩.   6. ♫♩.

These basic patterns should be understood as differently notated versions of familiar rhythms. To comprehend their ratio to the beat it is best to take every one of them through the different stages outlined below, keeping in mind that stages 2 and 2a are identical except that 2a is twice as fast as 2.

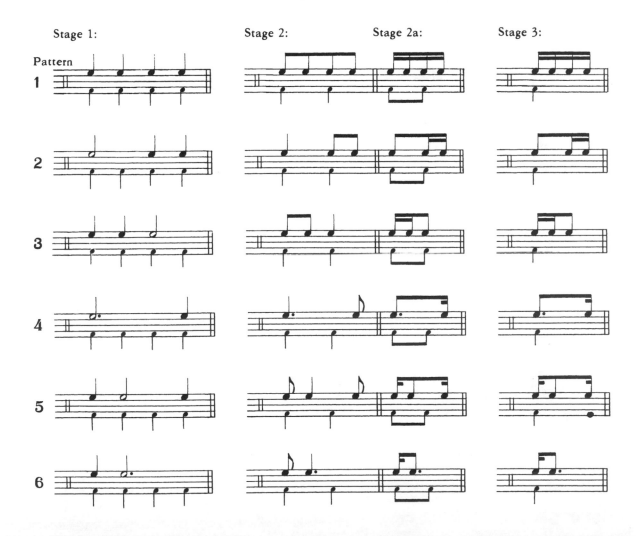

34

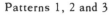Patterns 1, 2 and 3

Patterns 4, 5 and 6

The Sixteenth-Rest

Notation:

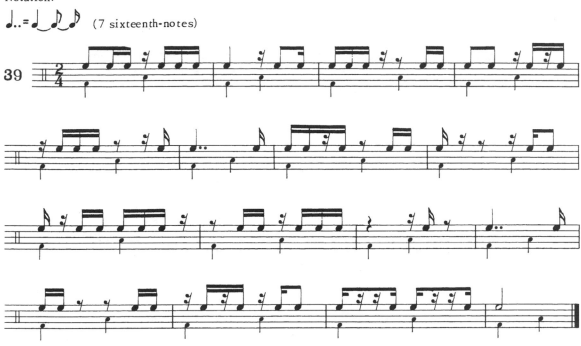

Upbeats using one or more sixteenth-notes occur frequently. To execute them precisely the pulse should be firmly established before beginning the exercise.

Sixteenth-notes can also be tied across the bar-line.

$\frac{2}{4}$ meter

$\begin{smallmatrix} 8 \\ 4 \end{smallmatrix}$ meter

42

$\frac{4}{4}$ meter

43

$\frac{5}{4}$ meter (3+2 and 2+3)

44

Changing Meters

Chapter V

Mixing Divisions of the Beat

The aim of this chapter is to practice switching back and forth between duple and triple divisions of the beat while maintaining an absolutely steady pulse. Each preliminary exercise should be practiced separately, perhaps preceded by ♩♩ ♩♩ and ♩♩♩ ♩♩♩

Preliminary exercises:

In order to perform certain more intricate patterns precisely, it may be necessary to subdivide the beat temporarily. For instance, when ♩♩♩ ♩♩♩ is followed by ♩.♩♩.♩ it is best to "feel" the four underlying sixteenth-notes.

Throughout this chapter these suggested subdivisions of the beat will be incorporated in the pulse line. The ability to temporarily subdivide the beat will become increasingly more important in later chapters.

$\frac{2}{4}$ meter

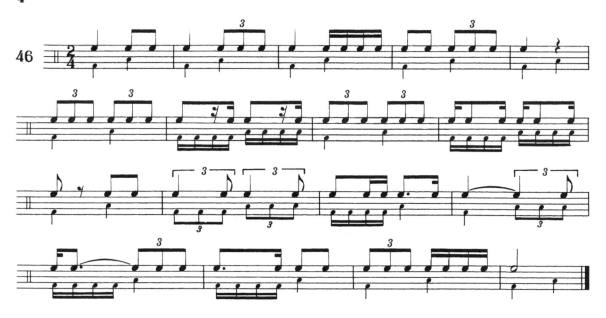

$\frac{6}{8}$ meter

Different notations have been used to divide the ♩.beat into two: ♪♪. or ♩ ♩ or ♪♪

Similarly, divisions of the ♩.beat into four may look like this: ♫♫. or ♫♫ or ♫♫

In this exercise the notations ♪♪. and ♫♫. are used.

$\frac{3}{4}$ meter

$\frac{9}{8}$ meter

In this exercise the notations ♩ ♩ and ♪♪♪♪ are used.

meter

$\frac{12}{8}$ meter

In this exercise the notations ♩♩ and ♪♪♪♪ are used.

Chapter VI

Dividing the Beat into Six Equal Parts

The Sixteenth-Note in the Triple Division

Basic patterns:

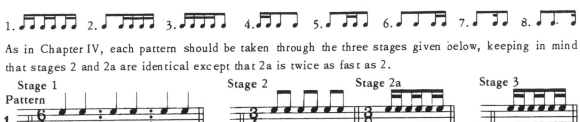

As in Chapter IV, each pattern should be taken through the three stages given below, keeping in mind that stages 2 and 2a are identical except that 2a is twice as fast as 2.

46

Patterns 1 through 4

52

Patterns 5 through 8

53

Eighth and sixteenth rests, ties across the bar-line, and upbeat.

With more intricate patterns, particularly syncopated ones not shown on page 45, a temporary subdivision of the beat is highly recommended.

48

The next four exercises may be practiced with an eighth-note pulse (♪♪♪ ♪♪♪) before they are done with a dotted quarter-note pulse (♩. ♩.).

Whenever the degree of difficulty warrants it, the suggested temporary divisions of the beat are indicated in parentheses.

$\frac{9}{8}$ meter

57

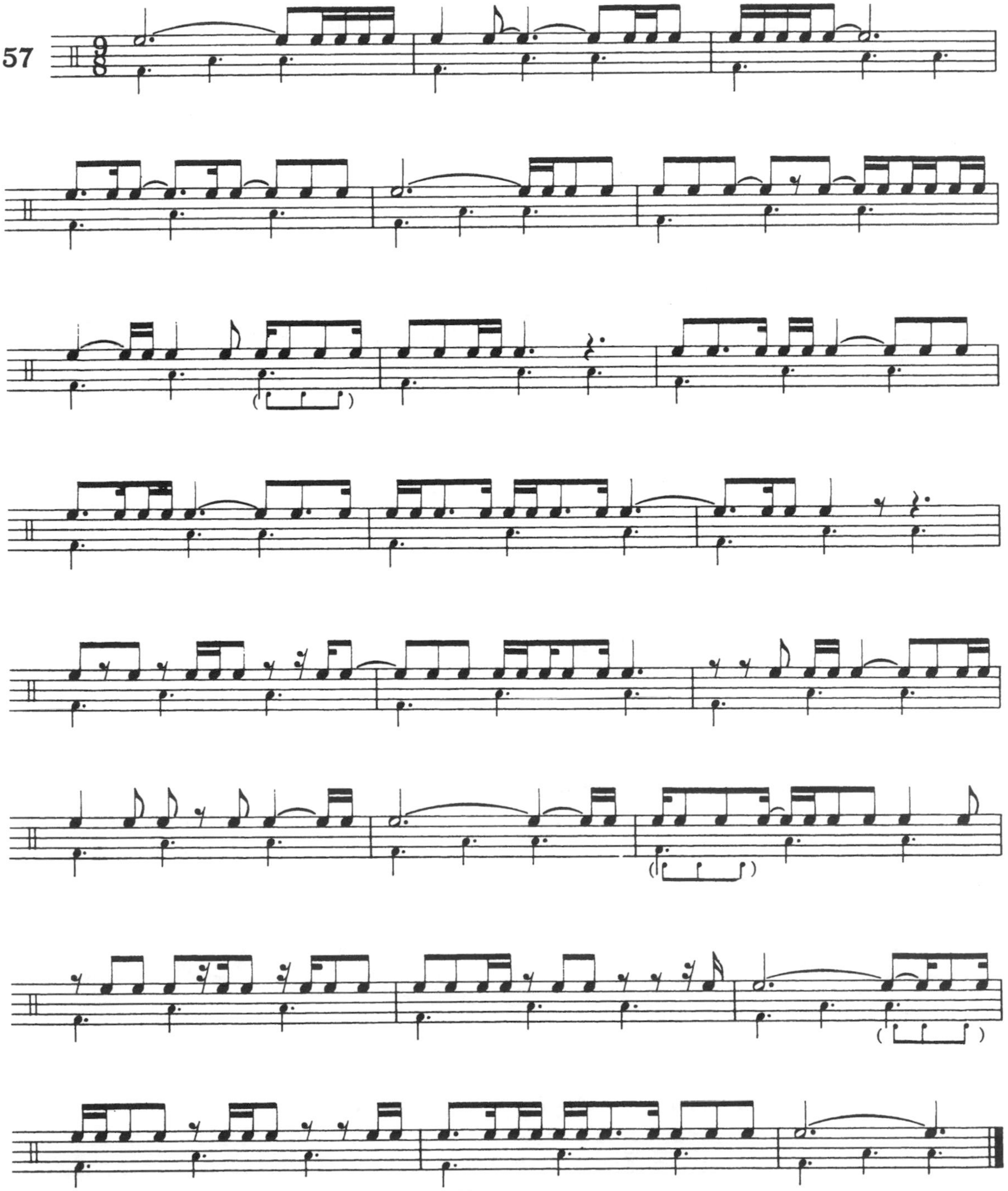

$\frac{12}{8}$ meter

58

451

Changing Meters

Chapter VII

Dividing the Beat into Five and Seven Equal Parts

When the beat is divided into five or seven equal parts no partial subdivision is possible. No combination of twos and threes will divide the beat into segments of equal duration.

Preliminary exercises

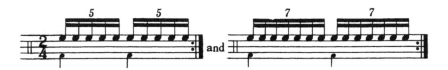

When more intricate figures are encountered, such as or the underlying beat itself must be subdivided, as explained in earlier chapters. and

The same applies to patterns involving division into seven or

Division into larger prime numbers: 11, 13, 17 etc. are occasionally found in Romantic music where they most often indicate "*rubato*" and do not need to be executed with precision.

The Quintuplet

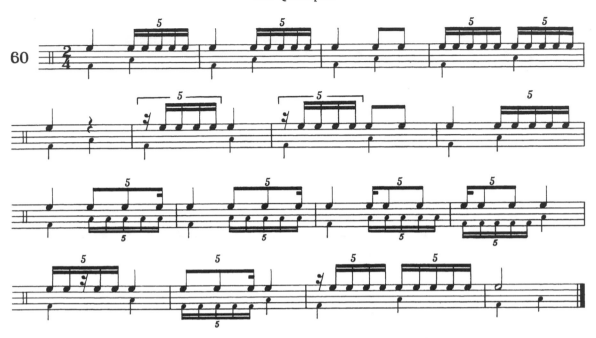

60

The Septuplet

61

Mixing divisions of 5 and 7

$\frac{2}{4}$ meter

$\frac{4}{4}$ meter

Chapter VIII

Dividing the Beat into Eight or Twelve Equal Parts

with the Half-Note (♩) as Pulse.

Since reading the smaller values is as much a visual challenge as it is a rhythmic one, dividing the beat into 8 or 12 should first be practiced with the half-note as pulse. As in previous chapters, the principle will be to temporarily subdivide the beat.

For instance:

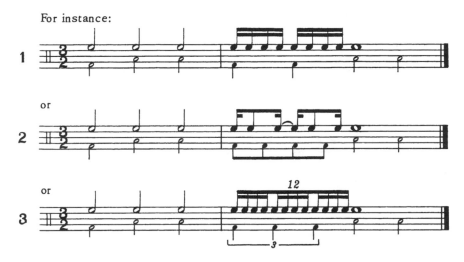

Since the essence of good sight-reading is looking ahead, anticipating the temporary subdivision of the pulse line by at least one beat will avoid sudden upsets and surprises:

Throughout this chapter these temporary subdivisions of the pulse will be indicated. Subdividing *every* beat should be avoided, since it will be no preparation for the succeeding two chapters.

Dividing the beat into 8

Dividing the beat into 12 .

Mixing divisions of 8 and 12

$\frac{2}{2}$ meter

$\frac{3}{2}$ meter

68

$\frac{4}{2}$ meter

* $\mathbf{o}$ = 4 beats

Chapter IX

Dividing the Beat into Eight, Twelve, Sixteen or more Equal Parts

with the Quarter-Note as Pulse.

Notation:

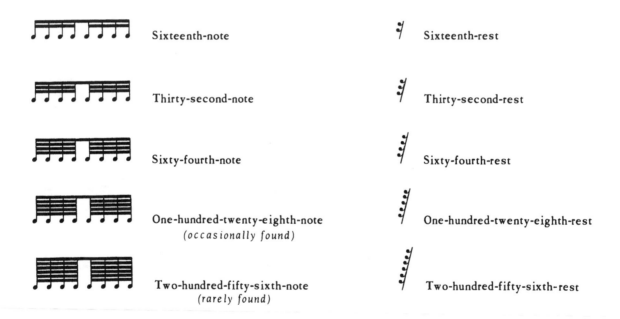

Sixteenth-note   Sixteenth-rest

Thirty-second-note   Thirty-second-rest

Sixty-fourth-note   Sixty-fourth-rest

One-hundred-twenty-eighth-note
(occasionally found)   One-hundred-twenty-eighth-rest

Two-hundred-fifty-sixth-note
(rarely found)   Two-hundred-fifty-sixth-rest

Some slow movements by Mozart and Beethoven are notated in these small values. Very often it is pos-sible to read the entire movement with the eighth-note as pulse, occasionally even with the sixteenth-note. In some movements, however, the basic pulse is the quarter-note. Then, when suddenly thirty-second-notes appear, it becomes necessary to subdivide the beat temporarily. In order to be prepared, it is best to sub-divide the beat immediately preceding the thirty-second-notes, as explained in the preceding chapter.

For instance:

PRELIMINARY EXERCISE

In this exercise the eighth-note is the pulse. The purpose is to get acquainted with the visual aspect of the smaller rhythmic values.

$\frac{3}{8}$ meter

The following eight exercises should not be begun without a glance at the smallest rhythmic values. In all music of this kind the maximum speed with which the smallest values can be performed determines the tempo for the entire piece.

4/4 meter

75

12/8 meter

76

Changing Meters

Changing Meters

Chapter X

Changing the Rate of Pulse

So far all the meter changes encountered were different counts of the same pulse. In much 20th-century music, meter change also involves a change in the pulse. For instance $\frac{4}{4}$ may be followed by $\frac{3}{8}$.

In this case the three eighth-notes are not a triplet; the duration of the eighth-note remains the same. This is often indicated in the music in the following manner:

Quarter-note pulse can also be followed by sixteenth-note pulse:

These changes in the pulse are practiced separately in exercises 79 and 80. The principle of anticipating the change of pulse in the beat immediately preceding it will again prove very helpful. For instance:

or

In both examples given, the quicker pulse was also continued for one beat after the second change of meter in order to re-establish the previous pulse firmly.

From ♩ pulse to ♪ pulse

From ♩ pulse to ♪ pulse

From ♩ pulse to ♪ pulse

From ♩ pulse to ♪ pulse

Chapter XI

SUMMARY AND REVIEW

In this chapter all previously practiced materials are mixed. The pulse and its suggested subdivisions are no longer given.

92

93

Chapter XII

Two Rhythms

Every pianist has to be able to perform two independent rhythmic lines simultaneously. In chamber music and ensemble playing this ability is of equal importance to performers of single-line instruments and singers.

In each of the preliminary exercises stage 1 (with subdivisions) should be practiced with increasing velocity until stage 2 (on a single beat) can be performed.

Preliminary Exercises:

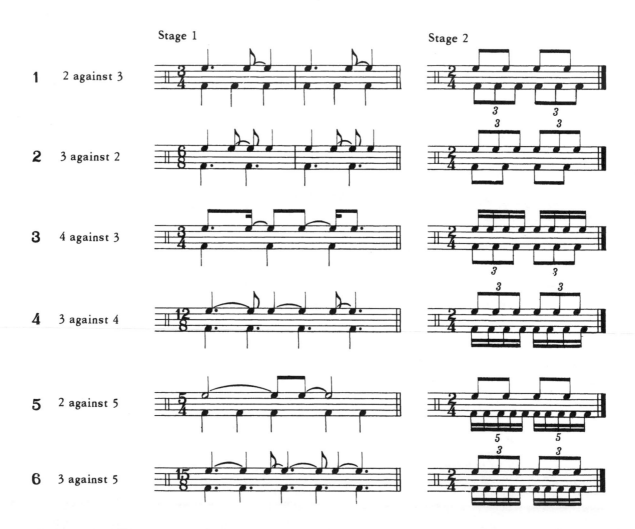

(Nos. 94 and 95 are rhythmic canons.)

94

95

96

97

99

100